Knowings from The Silence

Simple Wisdom for an Enlightened Life

Jim Larsen

Copyright © 2015 Jim Larsen
Knowings from Silence: Simple Wisdom for an Enlightened Life, 2nd edition
All rights reserved.
ISBN-ISBN: 978-0-9912920-5-9

This book is dedicated to Eva. Thank you for all the beautiful moments of Silence we shared.

The Silence...

The Silence is a proper noun, a tangible place. It is a place to visit, a place to go- a spiritual fortress, a meeting place of souls. It is the place you just were when you come back, not realizing that you had had been away.

The Silence is occupied by those who have found the doorways to it and enter without inhibition. These doorways are meditation, art, music, bliss, the absence of fear, the absence of worry. The ultimate truth of one's self is found in The Silence, in pieces, fragments.

The Silence is a finding place- a place to find the wisdom you need to be whole, dropped off by somebody before you who knew that someday a journeyer such as yourself would be along to find just such a thing- a piece to the puzzle of your personal truth.

Maybe in my truth, you will find a piece of your puzzle, a piece of your own truth. Maybe in yours, I will find a piece of mine. Isn't that why we write? Create art? Poetry? Music? Drama? Movies? Architecture? Why we run marathons? Break world records? Compete on the Price is Right? To inspire others and to share what we know?

Know that there are others. They are searching too.

They are asking questions too. Let them connect what they know to the pieces that you know. When enough people do this, what the world needs to know will be known. You will never personally know it all. How can you? How can anybody? Understand what is understandable to you because the ultimate truth can not be perceived by one person alone.

In each one's truth is a spark of another's truth. So read! Enjoy the arts; pursue your scientific or athletic endeavors, whatever it is that brings you the joy of living. Somewhere in that joy is the opening to your truth. Finding your truth will assist another and another and another and another in finding theirs.

Every one truth is a piece to a much bigger picture. The picture your puzzle puts together is but one piece of a much larger truth. Once all these truths are put together, what picture does it reveal? A picture of the greatness of the universe?

That is why we each must share what we know, what we understand, what has been revealed to us. Each is a piece of the puzzle. This is proof of the oneness of us all- even the trees, even the grass, every species of every being on the earth.

Consider the lessons you may learn from the observation of a single blade of grass. Through this observation you discover a truth. Share this truth. Another understands this truth and uses it as a

jumping off point to discover a truth of their own and

they share this. Every being is a teacher. Every being is a learner. Learn. Teach. Teach. Learn. It is a web. Thank that blade of grass for the lesson it provided. Thank the wind the sun the moon the stars the sky the clouds every being on this planet and beyond. There is an ultimate truth and the more we share with one another the closer we will get to it.

These truths are found in The Silence. Soften your heart and your mind so that you encounter no resistance upon entering. This softening occurs with bliss. What brings you bliss? Music? Athletics? Poetry? Meditation? Whatever it may be, use it as your entry point into The Silence. Once there, explore. Find. Contribute. What you find is yours to keep. What you leave behind may benefit another, so be generous in your offerings for they will help the universe expand and the human species to evolve.

Enjoy your time in The Silence. It is meant to be a joyous place.

Knowings: What is known by knowing, not by learning.

This book is a small collection of knowings. It is just a few things I found in The Silence. My hope is that somewhere in these pages you may find a piece of your own truth, that you may share that truth so that others may find pieces of theirs.

One's life's journey can be seen as a river to be crossed. There are a series of stones to jump from- one to the next until you reach the far side. How long will you remain on one individual stone before hopping to the next? Is there but one path of stones going straight across or are there many branches of stones going this way and that requiring a decision as to which way to go? Are the stones completely dry or are they slippery and wet? Are some stones seen with the eye yet under the water? Is it that you must wait for the water level to sink before jumping to the next stone? Will you in this given lifetime reach the far side of the river, or will you have to return to this river again?

It seems some people live their lives with their spirits densely packed within themselves. It's as if maybe they don't realize they have a choice. It seems that the more one spiritually awakens, the more their spirit wants to live outside of them, to reach for the divine in the other realms, and the divine in others, so it reaches out and out and out and out trying to connect. But those who are unaware often live with their spirit densely packed inside the shell of their bodies. But that is not where the spirit most wants to be. The spirit needs space. It needs room. It is singing "Don't Fence Me In." But the mind will entrap it. The mind sets blocks that prevent the spirit from being free. The mind, to one who is unaware of the spiritual way, is the supreme commander, the one with all the answers, the one who knows everything. Who is loudest is perceived as right. A screaming mind is hard to compete with. But it is not that spirit can't be heard. The spirit will not give up its endeavors to be heard or to break free of the mind's prison.

Sometimes we keep ourselves from achieving our greatest potential by long held, often long forgotten beliefs about ourselves that "we can't." But the reality is, yes we can. We just need to see that.

Whatever it is that you are trying to achieve, whatever it may be, if you feel a resistance inside of yourself, whether you can name it or not, or see it or not, or even feel it or not, take into consideration your desired outcome of this endeavor and give yourself permission to achieve it. Give yourself permission and then allow for the synchronicities that allow for it. Invoke your angels. Invoke your spirit guides. Invoke the presence of Jesus with his perfect love and say, "I give myself permission to…" "I give permission to my angels, my guides, Jesus, (and whoever else is meaningful to you) to dissolve all bocks keeping me from my success and my highest potential and to create the synchronicities that will take me to my success." And then allow for it.

Remember, your highest potential is your birthright. It is what you came to the earth to achieve. Any blocks to it are inorganic. They are in the way, whether you can see them or not.

Chances are you can not see them. This is a drawback to human form. We are too close to see. We do not have the bird's eye perspective that our team of angels and guides have. We trust that what our limited perspective does not perceive is known by our team. A good metaphor for this is when on the TV show Survivor when a team member wears a blindfold and another team member calls to them, telling which direction to turn as they steer the blindfolded one to objects to pick up. Consider this. There is much our team members see that we do not. Ask that they steer you towards them, and they will with absolute certainty. But you on Earth are required to do your part. Take the steps that are being called out to you. These are synchronicities. Do not shrug them off. They are real. Always. Honor them and honor your guides by following them.

Setting a goal and working towards it is great for feeling empowered, especially when feeling low.

Certain people act as bumpers in our life. They are deliberately placed in our path to propel us in a new direction when it is necessary to go in a new direction to achieve our highest and greatest good. They are synchronicities in human form who affect us in such a way that we make a very new decision based on how they affected us. This new decision alters the path your logical mind had put you on. This new path points you towards your purpose, as decided before you were born, towards your awakening.

By "Awakening" I mean the realization that our logical ego mind is not really in control after all. After our awakening, we may begin to recognize bumpers and appreciate them for what they are, even if, as people, you find them unpleasant and difficult to be around. This makes forgiveness so much easier.

Mistakes are what make a person great, for they are the greatest teachers offering the greatest lessons.

The idea that your life is planned out prior to your birth does not mean that everything, every single tiny detail of everything you think, do, and say in life is pre-scribed. It means the opportunities to learn and grow are in place.

Milestones. Our guides push us towards these milestones. We are all pushed in these directions and are given the opportunity to grow and to learn. Do we? Do we grow and learn from these milestones? Or do we backtrack, regress? It takes courage to learn, for to learn, we must forge forward beyond what is familiar.

It is so easy to stay in the comforts of familiarity, even when there are no lessons there, or the lessons there have been learned, rather than moving forward to what is next. It takes courage to move toward the light. The ego may not want to acknowledge a bumper for what it is. The ego may only fixate on the fact that this event or this person disrupted its perfectly laid out plan and now it's ruined.

The ego is stupid this way. Yes, stupid. What the ego needs to see is that this pain that you are experiencing is not a bad thing. It is a fantastic opportunity to forge new ground and to reach a new plateau. So tell the ego the shut up. Spirit must be louder than ego at this point.

Listen if you ever hope to hear what The Universe has much to tell you. Do not dictate the medium of the message. Allow for it in any form.

An awakened person knows that all is well and that all is good. An awakened person appreciates the guidance he receives and acknowledges it though gratitude. Do not underestimate the awesome power of simple gratitude. Saying "thank you" is all it takes to spark more and more blessings in your life. "Thank you" means you see and have experienced the blessings and synchronicities that are occurring and are now open to more. It is a wonderful thing. Be happy. It is okay to be happy. Where you are is always where you are supposed to be so be thankful for each step you take.

Perhaps we have a grand mission upon the earth. This mission is not confined to one lifetime. It could in fact, be stretched out lifetime after lifetime after lifetime after lifetime. When you come to the earth from wherever in the universe you originated from, you come with a mission. Perhaps your mission is to help the human species to evolve.

Perhaps one thing you do in one lifetime will affect you in another. Perhaps you will pick up on something from one lifetime, and continue it in another, or pick it up in the form of inspiration. Perhaps you were an artist or a musician in the past and this lifetime you are a fan or an admirer of what you did last time. As such, you are inspired to pick up on what this was and take it farther, or be opened spiritually by it. In this opening even more and/or greater divine energy comes through for you to share with human kind. Perhaps you were a singer in the past and in this lifetime the music of your past aligns your chakras to receive divine inspiration. Perhaps it is planned so that you receive from yourself in a time when you most need it to perpetrate your ultimate cause. This is something to consider when receiving inspiration from sources you most receive your inspiration from.

Perhaps the desire to manifest is simply you remembering what you planned for yourself, or your guides reminding you of this plan by creating a desire for it within you.

You are connected through the veil by the energy of your heart. Manifestation begins with the desires to be in a place or have a certain thing. This is you remembering your plan to be there or have that. Your efforts to manifest are part of the synchronicity that will align you with it.

A little awe and fascination of synchronicities and miracles is fine in the beginning, but then get over it and accept it all as part of your normal reality because it is and always has been. You are just now truly seeing it. But it's always been there. Treat that awe and amazement as a signal that you have awakened. Once awake, go on about your business.

The human race is poised for a great leap in evolution, but in order for it to happen; everybody needs to get on board.

Validation is a man made human conceit. It was never a part of the original design. The original intent created man to be self-sufficient in his ego. The ego was designed to serve the higher self, the spirit self as a means of action. But then the ego took over it was no longer content to be "just me." The needs of Spirit were in many to be forgotten and the ego needed more and more and many many "mores" after that to see it. This has been very unfortunate for the human race and detrimental to its evolution. A reversal is currently in engagement to bring human kind back to its original intention. This is Oneness. With Oneness, individuals will no longer need the ego validation of others, but rather the joining of spirit.

When you go through an unpleasant experience, remember the pain that it puts you through. Remember it that you may alchemize it into compassion for others in the future. Know that the hurt you are feeling will pass. It is easy to hide this pain with alcohol and drugs, but it is better to fully experience it and understand it to examine it and understand it in order to transmute it as compassion for others. To understand such pain is to witness it in others without judgment.

Compassion is understanding without judgment. Practice at it. It gets easy with practice.

We all have free will. Sometimes the goal can be to synchronize our free will.

Be an observer of your shadows. Do not get lost in them when exploring them. Keep a perspective on your shadows. To explore and understand, you must stand and/or rise above them to see them objectively if you wish to follow them to the source of their light. This is so. Observe your shadows and follow them to the source of their light to find what it is that brings you joy. Joy is bliss. Bliss is enlightenment.

The logical mind is imperfect. It does its best and when used properly, it is a good tool. So many people don't understand it though. So many people have no idea what to do with it. To master the logical mind is to master the universe.

As an empath, you may absorb a shard of energy from somebody. So, say you have absorbed this shard. This shard has its own vibrational energy. As such, this vibrational energy is attracting to itself more of the same energy. This shard, not being organic to you, you may not want this energy that is now being attracted. This can cause dis-ease.

It is so easy for the logical mind to categorize everything in terms of what is fair and what is not fair. The logical mind has this need to be all "Even Steven" about everything.

What a person should realize though, is that if they simply relax and let it go and allow for the natural flow of things, the Universe will balance it all out. Will the logical mind notice or be aware of this balancing out? Maybe it won't. This is where people run into trouble. They have such a need to know that everything is balancing out that they drive themselves crazy trying to see it. The trick is to surrender that need and simply trust that it is all happening as it should. If you can do that, life gets good.

Sometimes, all a person wants is to have the totality of the love they feel for somebody reflected back to them. When it is from the heart, there is a pureness about it. When it is from the head, it becomes obsession.

When you react in anger to something or some event, pay attention and try to understand this anger, for this anger represents something of yourself that is not yet healed.

Walk through your shadows to find what creates this anger. It is there. Do not condemn it or make it feel small, for that is not the purpose. The purpose is to heal it, for in healing we become strong. In becoming strong, we become complete. In becoming complete, we become enlightened. In becoming enlightened, we aid others in doing the same

Divine beings do not exist or operate in a linear fashion, therefore they do not view knowledge as progression. On the earth, we learn a little bit, build on it, learn a little more, build on it, learn a little more, build on it, learn a little more, build on it. This is a very linear view of learning. However, in the dimension of the divine, knowledge is holistic. Therefore, when divine shares knowledge they will likely share in a non-linear progression as pieces to a puzzle. Collect the pieces and put the puzzle together.

Anger blocks joy. Anger that has been suppressed is a silent killer of joy. You may not consciously feel the anger, but if it is in there, it will act as a shield never letting joy be experienced fully. Release the anger to be more complete in life. Do not take suppressed anger out on others. When you feel it rise, let it come to the surface and let it out. Observe it without pushing it back down. It serves you a great purpose to allow anger to rise and be put out so that it no longer binds you.

Relationships and love are about giving, not about taking. They are not about what you can get out of a person, but how you can enrich their life.

Love comes from the heart. It can only come from the heart. It is not an intellectual pursuit. It is a knowing. It is a knowingness. If it requires thought, it is not real. If you know it, it is real. A good relationship is one in which you and the other are equally willing to give, and to open to receive what the other is giving. Remember that giving is what makes the relationship strong, that is to say the other is strengthened by the giving process, and therefore it is imperative to their happiness and growth that you show gratitude and happily accept what they are offering.

A strong relationship consists of partners equally willing to give, with the only expectation is that the other will be enriched by it, and not what you yourself should receive in return. Let the other give what they have to offer. Accept it. Show gratitude for it. Be happy. This is a good relationship. Be sure the relationship is truly based on this mutual giving and receiving, and not about taking or being taken from.

One of the first steps on one's spiritual journey is to start asking questions. How do you know you are on a spiritual path? You know you are on a spiritual path because you notice things and you seek answers as to what they are and what these things are that you are experiencing.

Live your life on purpose with purpose.

Want to change your life? Start with your attitude. To live with an attitude of "I can't" or "this is impossible" means that it always will be impossible and that you never can. But to turn that around to an attitude of "I can do this" and "this is completely doable by me" opens the inevitability of the actualization of it. Be mindful of the Law of Attraction here. By saying "I can't" draws more of you not being capable. But saying "I can" draws to you more do-abilities to your life.

Witness the masks that people wear to hide their true selves. Why do they wear these masks? They wear these masks because they are secure in the attention they can get from others as long these masks are in place. They are unsure and uncertain of the attention they may receive from their own true authentic selves. To be aware of the masks others wear makes it possible to understand them and show understanding and compassion for them, aware that they wear these masks to hide insecurity.

Too often, we are at the mercy of the lowest common denominator- those who are un-selfaware.

Those that doubt- let them doubt. It doesn't mean you have to. Be a steward of your own truth. Be an ambassador of what you know. Be a tour guide of your intuition.

Evolution does not backtrack. Neither should spiritual development.

Turn your brain off, or at least give it a rest. It is getting in your way and not letting you experience the happiness or the joy that is your birthright on the planet. Your brain will instill fear over soul desires and needs and will shut the system down. Don't let your brain get in the way. If your heart says love, surrender and experience the joy that the love has to offer. Surrender. Your heart is infinitely more experienced in the knowing of these things. What has your brain ever done for you when pursuing or in a relationship besides given you fear worry or dread? Turn it off. If the heart is speaking then listen. Listen. Listen. Listen. Listen. Your logical mind will only screw it up and deprive you of what is meant to be and what could be and what should be. Why do that to yourself and to the other? Give in to joy. No brain work is required. Don't deprive yourself or the other of happiness.

Speaking words to somebody that will make them doubt their selves or shrink away is to plant the seeds of weeds in their hearts. Don't do that.

One way to gauge if you are learning the lessons you have set forth on the earth to learn is to examine if you still look for blame and fault, or do you accept what is.

Enlightenment is a series of awakenings. It is not a singular event. You awaken, you absorb the energy, you obtain the knowledge and the knowings, and when you take these to a higher plateau. You are now ready for your next awakening.

Thoughts become tangible forms within the mind and the body. They take shapes, sometimes blocks, sometimes daggers, sometimes wispy elusive clouds. If you do not like the way such a thought form feels, find it and remove it. It may need coaxing based on how rooted it is, but it is still possible to remove it.

"Please" "Thank you" "You're welcome" such simple words, yet so powerful in the amount of energy they provide the recipient.

Perhaps "enlightenment" is simply your ego finally realizing that you are worthy to call yourself one with God, acknowledging the perfection of the divinity that is within you.

Don't fall into the trap of excuses. An excuse is a trap your ego sets for your spirit to slow it down. Don't fall into them.

An inner child can so easily get lost in the shadows. Plunged into sudden darkness he may get lost. You may forget he is there. He will call to you wanting to be found, to be brought back to the light. Bring your inner child out of the darkness. It is a scary place for him and no place to wonder alone. You need your inner child in order to be whole. Your inner child supplies much clarity on complex issues involving the heart. If he is lost, find him. Do not let him be lost again.

So many people will live in such a way that is contrary to their greatest and highest good, and/or in ways that are unsupportive of their birth visions. This, of course, creates disharmony to the point of depression and frustration. They go to psychiatrists who help them to deal with the disharmony rather than address the fact that this disharmony exists. So instead of changing their life to be in harmony with their selves, they remain in disharmony and try to trick themselves into accepting it. Does it ever really work?

Jesus has already evolved. He is the cornerstone of human evolution. His perfect love is what the human race endeavors to emulate. Therefore, Jesus would never pass judgment on us. He does not condemn. He sees in us our perfect potential. He is a part of all of our teams and guides us, often silently, towards our personal light that will take us to our perfection.

The devil does not exist as an incarnate form. He exists in our personal doubts- our doubts that keep us from going toward our light. To beat the devil means to overcome these doubts about ourselves and get to the light. Doubt lies in ego. In our spirit, there is no ego. In our spirit, there is no doubt. How can there be? Our spirit knows of its own perfection and is perfect and therefore can not know doubt. Only the brain can know doubt and therefore the devil can only posses our brains.

If you are not exactly like everybody else, don't worry about it. You're really not missing anything.

People seem to have this idea that to be "enlightened" has something to do with light, as if being "enlightened" means being filled with some kind of light, divine light perhaps. I'm not saying that that is not the case. But I think it is more the case that "enlightened" more means to be made less heavy.

The ego and the mind will burden a soul, adding weight, weighing it down making it difficult and impossible to ascend. The soul is designed to ascend. To surrender the ego is to be made light. To become "enlightened" without the heaviness of the mind and the ego, the spirit is able to ascend.

Nobody is without the pain of sadness in their soul. The question is how close are you to somebody that you feel theirs? Are you able to soothe their pain? Their sadness? To be able to do this is love, compassion.

What you do to strengthen yourself spiritually in one lifetime will still be with you in others. Whatever you have done in the past, whatever vision quests or ceremonies that benefited you, whatever you did to strengthen your spirit and your connection to the divine, these benefits have remained. Likewise, what you do to strengthen your spirit and your connection to the divine in this lifetime will linger with you for all future lifetimes you will live.

The future is a lie because as of yet, it does not exist. When somebody speaks to you of the future, don't give them credence. They don't know what they are talking about. How can they? The future doesn't exist, not now, not ever. Ignore notions of it. It is a deceptive idea.

Love wants to flow. It is not meant to stay stuck. It is fluid. Building dams against it is foolish.

Think about what you want. Compare it to what you have. The difference is what you need to work on.

Life lessons that go untested may never be integrated. To integrate a lesson, step away from the environment in which you learned it. Does it have value in this new environment?

Being centered- this allows you to see all sides, the complete circle without obstructions.

Evil is to cause another to cast doubt upon themselves. Often, those who doubt themselves project this doubt onto others.

Imagine if we could experience one another purely as energy without regard to nationality, religion, race, gender, sexuality, physical attractiveness or lack there of, ego projection, and all manner of things such as that?

Transformation means cleansing. It means purifying. It won't always feel jolly and happy during the process, but when reflecting on the results, you appreciate it. Do not fear transformation for the physical unpleasantness.

To no longer seek, to simply be open to what you find- now that's a good way to live.

When somebody does something for you, they are giving you their energy. You should in return, give some of your energy by simply saying "thank you." But when you say "thank you" don't just say it as an intellectual logical thought process that you are supposed to do. It really has no meaning that way. That serves only to serve your own ego, giving you the chance to say, "Okay. I did what I was supposed to do." But that is not true gratitude. That's not even close to true gratitude. True gratitude comes from the heart. Find it in your heart, feel it in your heart, then say "Thank you." Otherwise, your words are just pointless, empty puffs of air that serve no one.

People will always respond to the potential they see in others.

What does that word mean though, "Awakening?" It means to become aware of the unique purpose of your life, or to realize that yes, you do have a unique purpose in your life. Maybe you don't exactly what that purpose is, but just the awareness that you came to the earth to accomplish something is an awakening in itself. Is it even possible to know the exact purpose you set for yourself when you were born? All you can really do is follow the synchronicities and your intuition and know that somewhere in it, following your bliss, that your purpose will be served. Trying to figure it all out and pinpoint the exact purpose really only serves the ego. The ego gets enough attention. Put it on the back burner and let your spirit just be free. Same with understanding your past life. Sure- it's interesting to speculate on past lives. I've done it, done it a lot, but what I really figured out is I'm up to this life now. This is the lifetime that makes a difference in the here and now. How about I just focus on what this life offers, and what I offer in this life? "Living in the Now" can mean so many things.

It is completely ridiculous to fake your emotions all the time. These people who always have a fake smile on their face acting like they are happy every minute when in reality they are not, are denying themselves the opportunity to explore what their true emotions are pointing towards. Our emotions are a guidance system for your spirit. To pretend to be only happy, to fake like nothing ever bothers you is like having a compass that doesn't have west on it.

An enlightened person will not force his or her ideas and attitudes on people, because when they do, they take the form of accoutrements of enlightenment rather than the reality of enlightenment itself. Rather, an enlightened person will offer his or her thoughts and ideas to those who ask and to those who will listen, but won't scream in their face about them. They won't force you to listen in the pursuit of ego gratification. They will offer their thoughts and the benefit of their experience for the honest benefit of others they see on the path.

To receive love, emanate love. Not from the head, but from the heart. What you put out into the universe is what you will attract. Put negativity out, you will receive negativity. Negative people will glom onto you. Put light and love out, and those are the people you will attract. Dispel negativity. It is harmful. It takes up space that could otherwise be taken up with light and love.

If you can't be with the one you love because the one you love does not love you, then love somebody else. This love is not authentic. It is a projection of your ego, your mind. Real love emanates from a softened heart to a softened heart. It is without effort.

So many people think in terms of "What went wrong?" When they should be thinking in terms of "What lesson does this teach me?" By looking for what went wrong they are looking for something to be wrong. By looking for something to be wrong they are looking to assign blame rather than accepting what is as an opportunity to learn. Don't assume its "wrong." Think in terms of this happened for the reason of allowing you to grow from it.

When desire/dreams collide with unwanted reality, scapegoats are often born.

The word "surrender" what does it mean exactly? It means to stop focusing your attention on that particular aspect of your self, most notably the ego and the mind- to cease production of the product that the mind and the ego produce worry, anger, fear, doubt, insecurity, sense of importance.

Tomorrow tomorrow tomorrow. Let's forget all about tomorrow. Let's make it today. Tomorrow has a way of interfering. Tomorrow has a way of getting in the way. Something is always lost in the translation of tomorrow. Focus on today. Today. Today. Today. There is no room for ambiguity when centered in the moment of today.

Disappointment happens when an expectation goes unmet. Eliminate expectations, and then it's all good.

People think of karma in terms of righting wrongs of past lifetimes or of learning lessons initiated in past lifetimes. Where to an extent this is an accurate assessment, it is better and more accurate to look upon this lifetime as an opportunity to set in motion that which will benefit you in future generations of your lifetimes on earth. Do good now. Follow your heart now. Listen to the voices now. By living in a right way now, you are putting into motion an opportunity to reap the benefits of right living in a lifetime to come.

Follow no prescribed spiritual path. Let the path you are on be blazed by you. Watch and observe. See what fits and incorporate those elements. Answer to no one but your own higher self. Share what you know but do not preach. If your knowings fit another's doctrine, that is wonderful. If it does not, that is fine as well. Seek no controversy, only acceptance and understanding.

Logic has limits. Logic has constraints. What is done spiritually, what is done "other wise" has not one single boundary.

We are separated from the Divine when we are on the earth. We feel that way. We feel separated and with that separation comes a longing to reconnect, to feel that perfect love. In each of us is a spark of that perfection. We are all perfect because we are all from Divine. In our earthly incarnations, we lose track of that feeling because of all the emotional baggage we pick up. But we all yearn to feel that wonderful connection to the Divine because that feeling is perfection. Because we each have that spark of Divine, we can find it in others. We can feel that perfection in others. This is why we are drawn to others. This is love.

Rejection only reminds us of the separation from the Divine. When you are with somebody special to you, you feel the connection to their spark of Divine, and thus you feel connected to the ultimate Divine. When that person, though, rejects you, pushes you away, makes you feel bad; it reminds you of how distant and separate you feel from the Divine.

It is true that different people operate from different inner places. Some operate from the head- always thinking, perhaps thinking "too much" they are probably prone to worry and to drive their selves crazy with their own thoughts. Others operate from libido, defining their selves by their connections with others, feeling inadequate when not in a relationship. It seems then that the most balanced place to operate from is right in the center of it all- the heart.

Everybody you encounter has their purpose. Honor their purpose by honoring them.

Your idea of what God can change as your needs change. If for a time your vision of God is that of an all loving entity who fills you with all the love you need so that you never feel a lack of love you have been seeking, that is in you and it is not going anywhere. Maybe that image of God has served its purpose for you. Perhaps now you need a God to show you miracles. Your idea of the God you need can change to a God who shows you miracles. This can happen and should. It shows evidence of personal evolution.

The heart will always be honest. The heart will always be true. Trust what the heart says. Learn to listen. Its message may not seem logical. This is because it is not based on logic. It is based on truth. Always trust the heart even when you do not see how its message can possibly be true. Trust that it is true, because it is. This is when it is important to soften your heart so it remains open. An open heart will be able to transmit its message much more easily than a hardened heart encased in cinderblocks of rigid thinking. By keeping the heart soft, you also allow for the manifestation of the message you are receiving, you are hearing. Questioning and doubting serve only to harden the heart, to solidify the cement keeping it encased. Do not do this.

Nobody has to settle for one source of abundance or another. The universe has it all for all. Never say you can't be rich and loved, or loved and rich, when both are attainable simultaneously. There is abundance for all.

Just as we as individuals must let go of concepts and ideas and attitudes that no longer serve us, so must mankind as a whole, through the collected consciousness of us all. But there are those in the collected that are unwilling to do this out of fear.

They must be led by example to an understanding and a knowing. Force will not make them understand. Force will only breed more fear inside of them. More fear will only slow them down.

Lead by example. Broadcast your message that it will be heard. But do not force it onto them. Let them come into it at their speed. The more you broadcast, the more they will hear. Before long they will start to listen.

Being "smart" is being able to do well on a test. Being "wise" is the realization that passing the test doesn't really matter.

Establish a baseline of who you are in terms of how you feel emotionally and spiritually. When you feel distressed or under pressure or that you have been pulled to another place that is uncomfortable to you, you have a destination to return to. Try if you can to make this baseline a place of joy and happiness. It is to your benefit to do this.

An empath must keep his or her feet on the ground, more so than most other people. They are much more susceptible to drifting away, carried by the thought forms of the others and the anothers. Empaths must be careful of this.

The brain has its purpose. Do not doubt the validity of this, the logical mind and the ego serve important functions. But those functions were never intended to interpret the messages of the heart. The heart has its own language. Applying the words and the concepts of the ego, the mind seldom works. Listen to the language of the heart. You hear it in the feelings you feel. So many of these feelings do not have words that describe them. The words from the mind that people so often use to interpret the heart serve only to limit the message. The message is not being heard from the lack of understandable communication. Strive to interpret the language of the heart.

The language of the heart is spoken through feelings. To understand this language, these feelings is to become a master of your destiny. From these feelings, life flows. When this flows, nothing remains stuck. Trust the message you receive. It is real and it is true. Flow with it.

What do want to achieve? Short term and long? Big small "impossible" do-able? Focus on it. Form it in your heart then push it to the universe without ever doubting. It is do-able. All is doable. It can and will happen. Allow it to. It is so much simpler than people give it credit for being. Give it a try.

If you are mad at me one day, do not carry that anger into the next. It is only weight that will slow you down. I will help you with this. I will make it easier by apologizing for whatever it is that I have done or perceived by you to have done.

Sometimes you need to hear advice and messages from people in words that you understand. Often, before this can happen, you need to develop your own vocabulary. While in the process of doing this, you may experience discomfort and even pain as you try to understand yourself so that others too will understand you. Don't judge yourself in this and remember to show yourself compassion.

Telling lies is counter productive to the manifestation process. The universe just doesn't quite know what to make of what you are trying to receive when your message is rooted in dishonesty. It is best not to lie, to yourself or to others.

Energy is exchanged among all living beings. This energy you put out is absorbed by others and for those who are empathetic by nature will surely have a strong sensation of this. The energy you put out is affected by a variety of factors, social conditioning, attitude, ego.

To become aware of the energy you put out, and the effect it has on others, whether empathetic or not, is a valuable tool towards conscious evolution of the species. How could it not be? If you hold onto gripes and grudges and let them manifest as anger, then you are putting that anger out there for others to absorb. Suddenly others are angry for reasons they may not be able to perceive.

This anger may magnetically attach itself to some mechanism within that person that is prone to causing anger, a long forgotten memory from childhood, perhaps, and then this person suddenly has anger building inside of them and in return puts that anger energy out into the world for still others to pick up. Imagine then, if a person where to put joy into the world for others to pick up.

"You're welcome" is just as powerful a force and an intention as gratitude, "Thank you." By saying "You're welcome" you are enabling the gratitude process of another. Don't underestimate this. When one is putting out the energy of gratitude to draw in abundance to their life, it is amplified when they know the gratitude has been well received. A heart-felt "You're welcome" accomplishes this.

The spirit may move forward, but the physical body encounters obstacles in trying to catch up. This is perceived as frustration.

One of the great benefits of humor is its effect on the mind and the ego. It forces the mind and the ego to stop for a moment and recognize its own ridiculousness and folly. Humor is a great bridge between the mind and the ego to the spirit.

All any of us really want is to be able to trust. This is where love comes from. The ability to trust and be trusted without fear of the trust being betrayed. We all seek to trust. It is a fundamental brick of existence.

Accepting and understanding and sharing for the good of others what is your natural talents and gifts is not an over action of the ego. Thinking that you are better than the others because of what you gifts provide is.

Begin each day by opening your heart to that day. Day by day heart openings- they will serve the universe a thousand fold.

The projections of others can easily become the masks and disguises we wear. What happens when we remove these masks, these disguises? Are we able to? What others expect from us, what they expect us to be for them and to them often distract us from our authentic selves. Of course, to an extent, defining ourselves as we are in the context of others is what creates the societies we live in. A balance must be established and maintained- a balance between who we really are and what our society needs us to be.

Echoes of the past, it is true, often reverberate in this now. We hear them in our worries and our fears, our phobias and our preoccupations. The echoes can also reverberate as bliss and as joy. A forgotten memory from a whole other now may be heard in a moment of causeless joy or of self-sustaining joy, triggered by seemingly nothing at all. But it's not nothing at all at all. It's something quite profound, in fact. It is the energy you created in that other now, still in the air. It is connecting in that other now, still in the air, with you of this now, as perhaps your thoughts, your actions or deeds in this now triggered a vibrational equivalent to the vibrational alignment you were in at the now of the original expression of this energy.

That previous now could easily have been in a lifetime previous to the one of this now. Consider this in figuring out your fears and your phobias, and in understanding patterns that repeat in your life, patterns that you feel may be blocking you in some way from achieving your birth vision for this time on earth. Trauma from one lifetime will inevitably ripple into your next lifetime, resulting in echoes.

You allow for miracles by noticing them, by acknowledging that they exist and that they happen as they happen. This way, you are open for more, allowing for more.

Thoughts are an articulation of reality.

To learn from your emotions, which are tremendously great teachers, observe them without reacting to them. Talk to your emotions. Ask them questions. Integrate them if you must, just figure out what lessons they have for you. If you find yourself reacting to your emotions, ask yourself why you are reacting this way? Remember too, often your reactions are contingent on social conditioning which is tied to ego. Often too, your reactions are based on your authentic self and what you are reflecting. Consider your soul, your authentic self as a mirror on which the surface of your emotions are reflected. If there is a piece of your soul missing, fragmented away somewhere, the reflection will be incomplete. Use your emotions as an indicator of what is missing so you can endeavor to find it. Remember, never deny a teacher. Never deny an opportunity to learn.

Accept challenges but never make excuses why something can't be done. The weak will tell you why they can't do something. Leave them to their dysfunction. Merely step around them and proceed to accomplish the task at hand. "Impossible" is a concept invented by and for the weak of mind and lazy of spirit to justify their own separate ego. It is a trap so easily fallen into.

The heart has no boundaries. The only thing it can not do is that what the ego tells it can not do, what the mind so convincingly suggests it can not do. In this way, this telling the heart what it can not do, the mind, the ego keeps the heart closed. It keeps the blocks around the heart rigid, and the cement binding the blocks strong. But when the heart realizes the fallacy of the mind, the ego, the light of the heart shines brighter, brighter and brighter until the cement holding the blocks together cracks and the blocks fall away. Now the heart is open. This is a heart that can do anything. Accomplish anything, because it does not know what it can not do.

By not slowing down, you force others to catch up to you. This, for them, is growth. As you try to catch up to another, this to you is growth.

For some, validation comes from finding and/or inventing invalidations of others and pointing at them proclaiming their inadequacies, thus validating their own selves. Do not give in to this.

The reason you must love yourself before others can expect to love you is because when you love yourself the charge of love is built up in you. This love emanates out and is felt by those around you. Their perception becomes, "It's okay to love this person" even if that is not articulated. This is the very basic Law of Attraction at its core. What you emanate finds like, and brings it to you. If you feel unsure or confused, you will bring more confusion. If you are sure, you will draw into you more surety. What you feel, what you emanate is what you will attract. So to find true love in your life, love yourself first.

If loving yourself is difficult, then there obstacles to overcome. These are not to be used as excuses, for an "excuse" is an unwillingness to try and to change. These blocks are merely mirrors. To not like what you see in the mirror means it is time to change your appearance. Change your appearance by changing your attitude.

Divine Grace operates through us all. Do not shirk away from the people who have a genuine need of what you offer. This is all part of the web that is existence on earth. Remember that the influence you have on others helps them to find the pieces of their puzzles that in return help others to find their own truths.

We are not perfect beings. No, we are human. Remember the ultimate and highest ambition s the growth and perfection of spirit. In human form, we are granted the unique and fascinating opportunity to explore the shortcomings and perhaps flaws of the spirit. To examine this and strive to perfect what we perceive to be less than desirable, we strengthen and enhance or spirits.

People often seek transformation with the hope that it happen instantaneously and may grow discouraged if it does not. Transformation however, is seldom an instantaneous happening. Transformation is a process. Processes take time. Those who allow for this time will greatly benefit and notice grand improvement in that which they seek to transform in their life. Those that are impatient for the transformation may not receive the full benefit of it through their impatience. They may not see the change they are hoping for as fast as they were hoping for and so their mind tells them that it is not working, that the transformation is not happening, and so they disallow the transformation.

Transformation, therefore, is not a product of the mind or the ego, although the mind and the ego will be affected by it. Transformation is in this sense, a spiritual pursuit. Remember, a caterpillar does not decide to become a butterfly, blinks its eyes and poof! Instantly becomes a butterfly. No, it must accept the process. It must accept the darkness of the cocoon.

Sometimes a person may find him/her self lost and trapped within their selves. With compassion, faith and understanding of others, perhaps they can be coaxed out into the universe where they can experience the true joy that is available to them and is their birthright.

One's spirituality should from time to time be tested. How else are you going to ascertain the strength and validity of it? Is untested spirituality nothing more than dogma?

Imagine unlearned lessons and growth experiences as tangible objects taking up space within you. Imagine that the majority of your energy is going towards dealing with this old stuff. Wouldn't that energy be of better use if applied toward new growth instead of dealing with the old? This old stuff is spiritual clutter. Burn through it so that it is not holding you back and preventing new growth.

Observe your ego and appreciate the humor it provides. Laugh. Laugh at your own ego and the expectations it has.

Sometimes you have to get to where there are no expectations of you. This way you can become what you need to be.

The absolute worst thing you can do to yourself is convince yourself that you know all that you need to know. There is so much more to learn, to understand. Never deny a teacher. Don't let ego block you from wisdom. Don't let ego convince you that a particular being has nothing to teach. You are denying yourself and others and thus the universe when you do this.

Things are important to the extent that we place importance on them. No more. No less.

Intuition is pure, perfect knowledge because it is a direct communication from spirit. The mind will muddle it if allowed to. Practice listening to intuition without interpretation from the mind.

Art- all art, the medium does not matter, is an opening to other worlds, a chance to see beyond the veils that separate so many different realities. Be open to the art that moves you. Allow it to take you to other worlds, for that is what it is designed to do. Allow for it.

Don't be afraid to communicate with others. If it is in your heart, know that it did not get there by mere coincidence. What you find in your heart is organic to who you are and more importantly, why you are. Do not fear what you find in your heart. What is in your heart was placed there by your spirit. It is your spirit. So explore the unexplored regions. See what is there. Know that it is true and real and that when shared with others, the others will know the realness of it and appreciate it. Much of what is there, in your heart, is there to be known by others. Share. Trust. Know. Be fearless.

Life begins when you develop an awareness of the masks you have been wearing, and find both the courage and the strength to remove them.

So much knowledge is so simple. It is right there in front of us, right there within us. So often, we look beyond ourselves for the knowledge that is within us. We look for answers from beyond, but if we look within, there they are- the answers.

One who thinks they know everything, or that there is nothing more to learn, has the most to learn, and will likely do so through pain and difficulty.

Be sensitive to the energies of other people. Use what you feel from them to understand them and to understand yourself as well as you examine your reaction and you interpretations of these people and their energy. Do not, however, use what you feel of their energy as a prompt to judge them or yourself. Simply observe and learn what there is to be learned.

An open heart will greatly enhance your creative output and abilities. When you are creating from the heart, this is pure creation from your spirit. When creating from the mind, it is often a creation from the ego, often to mask and to cover pain. Keep your heart open to be truly creative.

A person may be drawn to another based on what they see of themselves reflected in this other person. When there is a soul fragment missing in the person is drawn to, then it is as if they are seeing themselves in a broken mirror. It is important to undergo soul retrieval so that you are whole, of course, but also for those who see themselves reflected in you. They need to see the whole, undistorted image. To love one's self is to appreciate the wholeness of one's self. This is another reason why it is important to love one's self, so that one is as a complete reflection of the other as possible.

Use empathy as a healing tool. Strive to not be buried by the feelings and emotions of others, but rather to feel what they feel, and use that to identify blockages that they may have, and help them to overcome these blockages.

Perhaps enlightenment is the attainment of complete sureness of self- to not feel doubt or worry, to appreciate one's own perfection and to know it and see it in others even when, especially when they do not see it in their selves. To not question or doubt one's self.

Honor the perfection you see in others even when they don't see it in their selves, because in your reflection, perhaps they may see it for the first time.

Seek to bring forth the good qualities of a person that their life will benefit from it, not yours. Allow the benefit of this act to come to you through empathy. Don't seek it or attempt to force it. Allow it to flow to you.

The main reason for not achieving a goal or living up to your potential is simply for not allowing yourself to. This is the ego exerting its control. The ego thinks it knows what you can and can't do, should do, should not do, are able to do, unable to do. It convinces itself that you are unable to achieve certain goals and does all it can to make this the reality. Ignore the ego's voice of negativity. Accomplish despite the ego's insistence that you can not. The more you beat the ego in this way, the weaker the ego's hold becomes until spirit has the loudest voice.

Sometimes our impulses are a synchronistic inspiration placed in us by the manifestation desire of another. It is so that for this person's manifestation to be accomplished, you are necessary. This relates to oneness.

Sometimes we seek to understand ourselves by applying what we see in others, what we perceive and generally understand of others, and in those who have come before us, to ourselves. While in many cases universal truths can be applied in this way, it does not allow for the acceptance and understanding that much of who we are, we bring with us in spirit form. Much of our earthly existence is who we are in spirit. Your spirit may come from a place that is separate and distant from those that you compare yourself to. Allow your understanding to follow from a place that is unique to you. In this, much of who you are is unique. Your understanding of yourself must take this into account.

Much of who you are can not be compared to others. Much of who you are is just you. Accept this. It is a good trait that is the quality of who you are and what you know and contribute. Deposit this into The Silence for the others. It will greatly be of benefit.

Untested beliefs- this is why we debate, to test our beliefs and examine the validity of them in the context of opposition.

People who don't know what they can't do tend to do some pretty amazing things.

Love is not an obsession. Love is not of the mind. Love is a passion and a compassion. Love is a mutually acceptable empathy. Love is not a mindset. Love is a setting of the heart. Love is a flowing of the heart.

More often than not, humor is simply telling the truth without tempering it. Most people are so unaccustomed to hearing the truth stated so bluntly and so simply that to hear it this way is startling to hear. So often we temper the truth because the truth seems too harsh. The untempered truth will often make people laugh.

The goal sometimes is not to fit in and conform to others, but to be comfortable with yourselfwho you are, no matter what the discrepancies are between you and others who represent a situational "norm."

A failure is simply somebody who is unable to, or is unwilling to see and/or identify the lessons that any given situation, particularly a setback, has to offer.

Experiencing pain, emotional pain can lead a person to stagnate themselves. Having experienced this pain, they may be reluctant to put themselves back into the situation that caused this pain. This has the drawback of disallowing yourself to experience other possible outcomes.

There are infinite outcomes to any given situation. If you are reluctant to put yourself back into the situation that caused the pain, you are denying yourself the opportunity to experience another outcome. What is the root of this fear? This fear of re-examining this fear? Disappointment.

It is likely that you had a hope, an expectation of a desired outcome of the situation. This outcome, however, did not come to pass. Something quite the polar opposite was the actual result. Likely, this polar opposite outcome caused emotional pain.

It is natural to be reluctant to put yourself in the position to experience that again. But to grow, experience the new, you must acknowledge this fear and then transcend it. To not do so means to stay in a state of stagnation and not see in the distance, new horizons and the sun rising over new plateaus.

One who does not show gratitude, who does not offer the simple offering of "thank you" to let somebody or some divine force know that their energy was received and appreciated is somebody who has not yet awakened, for when one is awakened, they become aware of the energy of others, and knows that their own energy interacts and affects the energy of others. One who has awakened has compassion for these others and will provide for them, empathetically, simple gratitude to give their energy that boost that comes with appreciation. One who has awakened will never pass an opportunity to express gratitude, knowing that to show gratitude is to invite more abundance into their life.

By The Law of Attraction, you will find what you are looking for. If what you are looking for is an excuse why something is impossible, then it will always be impossible.

Keep in mind and remember that the earth is a wonderful place with much to experience, appreciate, and learn. Some lessons are joyful, others painful, but the end result is the same-enlightenment.

Remember to be present on the earth. Look to the Divine for help, comfort and compassion, but do not dwell there. You are welcome to peek there and visit there. This is encouraged for the guidance it provides, but you are on the earth to experience the earth as earthly beings. Enjoy it. Enjoy the joy of it. Appreciate the pain of it for what the pain offers- lessons and growth.

We distinguish between "spiritual" and "earthly" or "mundane" because the logical mind needs control. We see them as two distinct entities or life forces. There are others who make no such distinction because the logical mind, their logical mind, surrenders control. They do not need to differentiate what is spiritual and what is mundane because to them all that matters is the holistic nature of it all.

When the logical mind gets out of the way, only then do miracles happen. Sometimes getting the logical mind out of the way is a miracle in itself.

Your conscious mind may only attach minimal connection to another being on the planet, but that does not mean on the level of spirit, the connection may be much more profound and significant. Remember this.

We create our own reality. Yes. This is true. It happens though that sometimes we are seemingly trapped in a reality created jointly by others that have little or no bearing on a reality that we ourselves would create. This can lead to disappointment and frustration.

Disappointment and frustration, of course are constructs of the mind, the ego. What then do we do to create a paradigm that is in more of an alignment with the reality our spirit needs? We create a reality of our own no matter what. If this so called reality that you find yourself in that is incongruent with your needs is not desirable to you, remember, you put yourself there for a reason. Perhaps that reason is that being there allows you to explore hidden contents of your character. Perhaps this is the best opportunity you have to explore your shadow side or to find within yourself reserves that you did not know you had but serve you well in the building of the content of character you came to earth to build. Nothing is for nothing. Explore this collected reality you are in. If it is dark to you, find in yourself the light.

As you find reserves to cope with this, to you, unpleasant reality, so may others; others too may be finding reserves to cope with your reality that may be unpleasant or challenging to them. Keep this mind- dual realities. It is easier, yes, to be with like minded people who are aware of such concepts as reality creation, but to be alone in a world of those unaware of the dream can have the benefits of finding strength. Strength found can never be lost or squandered.

It is important to change your attitude from "Wanna Be" to "Doer." A "Wanna Be" lacks the conviction to get it done. A "Wanna Be" sees himself/herself as standing outside the door of their dream, looking in wishing they had an invitation to walk through the door and enter into the world of dream fulfillment.

A "Doer" doesn't wait for that invitation. He/she just walks right on in and announces to all present, "Here I am!" It really is all about attitude. Don't ever forget that. Change your mind-set, change your life. It is true in every aspect. Don't believe that? Try it and see.

Learning equals growth and expansion. If you think you know it all already, you are stagnating yourself.

A person may wear a mask for the purpose of transformation. A person may set their intention that they will become this other person, a better person than what they perceive their selves to currently be, so they wear the mask of this other person. At first, the mask may seem to others to be unnatural, phony. But to a person dedicated to living this change, the mask will not remain a mask. To a person dedicated to making this change in their life, the mask will become their true face. This is a different kind of mask than those who wear masks to facilitate denial.

The ego needs to know how, when, and why. Spirit simply says, "It shall be."

You have one very distinct advantage in life, and that is, you are you, and with that you bring to every situation your unique set of experiences from all you have collected from this life as well as the many lives you have lived previously. Think about that.

Your unique wisdom and knowings will give you the advantage in any situation. The trick is to see your uniqueness, to identify your unique knowings and knowing how to apply it. It will benefit you, it will benefit human kind. As you apply what you know, you expand the awareness of the situation many fold. As it expands it will touch others. They will apply their unique knowings to it in a likewise fashion. This is wisdom. This is the growth of knowledge. This is the evolution of the human species. You are responsible for it. You make it happen. In this way, you are amazing. In this way, you have a distinct advantage- you are you.

Suspend all agendas. Cancel all plans. What then fills in the gaps is the truth of who you are.

"Justice" is a manmade concept. It has no bearing in a universe of forgiveness. The universe seeks only balance.

You can read the ideas of others as much as you want, but unless it resonates with you, it is not really knowledge.

Only when you are awakened do you begin the search for answers. The unawakened drift through their lifetime oblivious to the grander scheme that this lifetime is about. But do not judge. Perhaps they are gathering strength, knowledge, understanding and clues that they will bring back with them in their next lifetime.

For an enlightened person, life need not be lived in chronological order.

Explore your boundaries. Find where they are and go beyond them. Scary? At first, sure. But the farther away you travel from them the easier the journey becomes until you forget those boundaries ever existed at all which reveals them to be what they are- artificial constraints designed by the ego to keep itself from having to redefine itself.

Do you judge yourself or simply observe your feelings concerning whatever is at hand, and observe your reaction to your observation? Do not fall into the trap of judging yourself on your reactions to your observations. Your reactions are valid. If they make you uncomfortable or you do not like what you see in your observations of your reactions, perhaps this is an area you need to work on in achieving your goals and personal evolution.

Everybody has their own thing going on in their life in this lifetime. Maybe it is for some to heal and to help others, but for others it could just to learn a seemingly simple lesson. Maybe to do this, to learn this lesson, they need to be homeless, or seemingly asinine or undesirable to others. But whatever it is, they are learning. Perhaps in a previous life, they got to within a breath of perfect enlightenment, but before that enlightenment can happen, they must still learn this minute lesson. This could easily be the case. So who are any of us to judge?

Peel away the layers of masks and social conditioning to reveal the truth of who you are before you can expect to make true friends. Otherwise, you are attracting people to you based on false premises. Likely the untruth of your mask is attracting the untruth of their mask, never knowing the truth beneath theirs, nor showing the truth beneath yours. This is a life of falseness and hardly a life at all.

Sometimes, we live based on the memory of an emotion. We have to remind ourselves that this is all it is- a memory, otherwise it can easily hold us back.

Words are meaningless unless they come from the heart. Therefore, it is so that one's heart must be pure and in good emotional and spiritual condition to be of value to the words spoken. The condition of the heart will affect the words spoken from there. However, if the heart speaking the words is wounded, be mindful that you may assist in the healing.

A step towards getting over unreasonable fear is to learn and be able to trust. When you are able to trust and the trust you have is not betrayed, your energy is not going towards fear of betrayal, but rather more uplifting and positive things. This is why we must live as trustworthy beings, so that others may be enriched by the trust they have in us.

Also By Jim Larsen

Knowings from The Silence vol. 2: More Simple Wisdom for an Enlightened Life

Knowings from The Silence vol. 3 Even More Simple Wisdom for an Enlightened Life

What's Tarot Got to Do With It? The Fool's Path to Enlightenment

The Double Oh Fool Guide to Tarot Mastery

Fat Naked Poetry

Poetic Deviance

www.foolspathtarot.com
www.byjimlarsen.com

www.ingramcontent.com/pod-product-compliance
Lightning Source LLC
Chambersburg PA
CBHW071504040426
42444CB00008B/1490